A'S NATIONAL PARKS

THE CIVIL WAR

Troops skirmish at the Second Battle of Bull Run, lithograph by Currier & Ives.

WRITTEN BY ROBERT K. SUTTON

Copyright 2014 by Eastern National
470 Maryland Drive, Suite 1, Fort Washington, PA 19034
Visit us at www.eParks.com

The America's National Parks Press series is produced by Eastern National, a
not-for-profit partner of the National Park Service. Our mission is to promote the
public's understanding and support of America's national parks and other public trust
partners by providing quality educational experiences, products, and services.

ISBN 978-1-59091-162-4

Civil war is one of those strange terms in the English language that does not seem to make sense. The definitions of "civil" are: "of or relating to ordinary citizens and their concerns," or "courteous and polite." The definition of "war" is simpler: "an armed conflict between two parties." When put together, civil war is "an armed conflict between citizens of the same country." A civil war, like any other war, often begins with the leaders believing that it will be over quickly, and that whatever goals they wish to achieve will be gained without much bloodshed. Once any war begins, however, there is no way to know how long it will last, which side will win, or how many lives will be lost.

At the beginning of the American Civil War, many on both sides believed the war would last a very short time and that their goals could be achieved quickly and with little bloodshed. Instead, the war lasted four long years, and about 750,000 Americans lost their lives. In fact, more Americans died in the Civil War than all other American wars combined.

What caused the American Civil War?

Civil wars may begin when one tribe doesn't like another tribe; when one religious group does not like another; when there is a conflict over land or resources, or something else. The something else that caused the American Civil War was the institution of slavery. When our nation was formed, our constitution recognized and protected the right to own slaves. Even then, many Americans were opposed to slavery, but, in order to unite the nation, our founding fathers agreed to allow slavery to exist. They

Left: Confederate soldiers pose for a photograph.

Slaves pick cotton on a Southern plantation, 1850 engraving.

agreed because slavery was either abolished or declining in the northern states, and they hoped that slavery would eventually end throughout the country.

In time, with favorable land and climate in the South, and with new processing equipment, cotton became an important and valuable crop. Cotton fueled the industrial revolution in Europe and the northern United States, and these factories could process as much cotton as the South could produce. In 1830, the South exported 720,000 bales of cotton. By 1850, that number swelled to 2.85 million bales, and by 1860, over five million bales were shipped from cotton-growing states, making up more than 60 percent of all United States' exports, and valued at more than $200 million. By 1860, on the eve of the Civil War, there were nearly 4,000,000 enslaved people in the United States, and their monetary value was greater than all of the factories, banks, and railroads combined.

As the demand for cotton and the demand for slave labor to produce cotton increased, agitation in the North from a growing number of reformers to abolish the institution of slavery increased as well. Opposition took different forms. Some wanted to end slavery immediately, allowing all enslaved people complete freedom. Others proposed gradual abolition, where parents would remain slaves, but children would be free. Others favored the African colonization program, where slaves were either purchased from or released by their owners and sent back to Africa where they would live their new lives in freedom.

But the slave states were determined to protect their growing wealth and vast economic investment in slavery, and to protect a way of life that ensured that both free blacks and slaves were subordinate to white people.

To try to balance these interests, Congress created a series of compromises that didn't please everyone but maintained the peace. In 1820, the Missouri Compromise admitted Missouri as a slave state, Maine as a free state, and established the policy that any state admitted below the southern border of Missouri would be slave, and any above would be free. The Compromise of 1850 admitted California as a free state—although most of the state was below the southern border of Missouri—and passed a very strict Fugitive Slave Law that made it much easier for slave owners to capture and return their runaway slaves to servitude, even if they had managed to escape to free states.

In 1854, the Kansas-Nebraska Act allowed the residents of Kansas and Nebraska territories to decide for themselves whether or not they wanted slavery. Proslavery and antislavery forces clashed in what was called

Proslavery Missourians on their way to plunder and burn the capital of Lawrence, Kansas, in 1856.

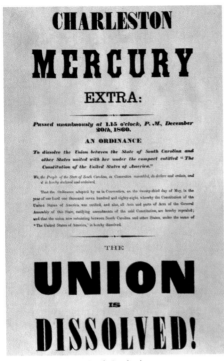

Broadside announcing South Carolina's adoption of an ordinance of secession.

"Bleeding Kansas" before Kansas was eventually admitted as a free state. Finally, in 1857, the Supreme Court stepped in. In the case of *Dred Scott v. Sandford*, the court decided that Dred Scott, an enslaved man who was claiming his freedom because he had been taken to a free state, was still a slave. The court went much further, however, and declared that all African Americans —free or slave—were not citizens, and thus did not have the right to vote or bring cases before the courts. It further ruled that Congress did not have the power to restrict slave owners from taking their slaves into any American territories.

The Dred Scott Decision was too much for most Northerners, who did not like the institution of slavery, but were willing to allow it to exist where it was. Many, however, drew the line there, and vowed to fight any efforts to allow slavery to expand into western territories. On the other hand, when Abraham Lincoln was elected president in 1860 on a platform stating that slavery could continue in the states where it existed in 1860, but would not be allowed to expand into any new territories or future states, this became too much for many Southerners.

Not long after the presidential election of 1860, 11 states, starting with South Carolina in December 1860, seceded (withdrew) from the Union, creating the Confederate States of America. As this new government was created, Alexander Stephens, its new vice president, explained why the South left the Union. "The new [Confederate] Constitution has put at rest forever all the agitating questions relating to our peculiar institution—

The North Builds an Army

Though the United States had a trained officer corps and standing army and navy, the last war was fought in 1848 against Mexico. Since that time, the small army had been scattered to forts throughout the trans-Mississippi West. Many of the officers who had served in Mexico were almost retirement age or past; many were from the South, and when war came chose to resign and return to their native states. Lincoln's April 1861 call for 75,000 volunteers to defend the Union was followed by another in May for 42,000 men. In addition to enlisting men, the Union had to equip and train them. The states also raised and equipped units. The results were mixed, especially when it came to uniforms. Originally, there was no standard, and troops went into battle clad in blue, gray, black, and red. The Union quickly settled on blue. In early 1861, the United States Army consisted of fewer than 20,000 men. By the time Lee surrendered at Appomattox Court House in 1865, more than 2.5 million men had served.

Union soldiers photographed with muskets and a drum.

African slavery as it exists among us—the proper status of the negro in our form of civilization," he said. He went on to say that the Confederate government's "foundations are laid, its cornerstone rests, upon the great truth that the negro is not equal to the white man; that slavery, subordination to the superior race, is his natural and moral condition." He left no doubt that slavery was the reason for the South leaving the Union. The North considered Southern secession an unconstitutional act of rebellion, and entered the war with the aim of reuniting the Union. When asked what his object was in fighting the Civil War, President Abraham Lincoln wrote in an August 22, 1862 letter to Horace Greeley, an influential Northern newspaperman, that "my paramount object in this struggle is to save the Union, and is not either to save or to destroy slavery. If I could save the Union without freeing any slave I would do it, and if I could save it by freeing all the slaves I would do it; and if I could save it by freeing some and leaving others alone I would also do that."

The War Begins

Early on, many leaders—especially those in the Confederacy—thought if there was any fighting, it would be brief and relatively bloodless. A.W. Venable, a secessionist from North Carolina, said he would "wipe up every drop of blood shed in the war with [a] handkerchief of mine." Senator James Chestnut, Jr., from South Carolina offered to drink all of the blood spilled in the upcoming conflict. Indeed, if the bloodshed resulting from the first military encounter at Fort Sumter in Charleston Harbor, South Carolina, was any indication, they would have been correct.

The Confederates attacked the Union army holding out at Fort Sumter on April 12, 1861, and after 30 hours of bombardment, the Union army surrendered the fort. Two men died from accidental causes rather than the direct shelling. There were other engagements, but the first major land battle took place just 25 miles from Washington, D.C., near a stream called Bull Run and a railroad junction called Manassas. The Confederate army had set up a defensive position along Bull Run mostly to protect the rail lines,

The Confederate battery at Fort Moultrie firing on Fort Sumter, lithograph by Currier & Ives.

and the Union army attacked, in part to capture the railroad junction and in part to continue to Richmond, Virginia, to capture the Confederate capital.

The Battle of Manassas (the Confederate name for the battle) or Bull Run (the Union name for the battle) was very different from Fort Sumter. Spectators from both sides came out to watch; some even brought picnic lunches. For the first time in world history, troops were transported by railroad to fight in the battle.

In the battle, both sides were nearly even—about 35,000 on each side— but few soldiers on either side had ever been in a battle before. What became known as First Manassas or First Bull Run (there was another battle on the same ground a year later) dispelled any notion that this would be a bloodless war. The Confederates won the battle, convincingly, but there were some 5,000 combined casualties, of which 900 were killed, making this the bloodiest battle in American history to that point.

Several things were revealed at Bull Run. The new rifled muskets that many on both sides used fired lead bullets that were far more effective and easier to load and fire than any before. A good sharpshooter could hit a target at about 700 yards, which changed many assumptions of warfare. Artillery soldiers in earlier wars were far enough away from the close combat fighting, and they generally were in safe positions. With the rifled muskets, members of artillery crews were now vulnerable. Cavalry charges were rare, because the range of Civil War muskets could pick off horses and riders well before they could charge. Early in the war, one side would launch a frontal assault on the other side, often with devastating losses for the attacking side. As the war rolled on, the construction of protective trenches became more and more common; frontal assaults were less and less common.

A slave family's sighting of Union army lines, 1863 illustration by Edwin Forbes.

The number of deaths in the Civil War is a frightening number by almost any standard of measure. But, compared to earlier wars, the numbers of soldiers who died from their wounds were actually lower. Ether and chloroform used as anesthesia for surgeries—mostly amputations—saved numerous lives that would have been lost in earlier wars when patients went into shock. Sanitation in camps improved, but still two Union and Confederate soldiers died from disease for every one killed in combat. In the Napoleonic Wars, the ratio was eight to one, and in the Crimean War, just a decade earlier, the ratio was four to one.

Slowly but surely, the war for the Union also became a war for freedom for American slaves. On May 23, 1861, barely a month after the attack on Fort Sumter, Frank Baker, Shepard Mallory, and James Townsend, three enslaved men forced to work on a Confederate gun emplacement near the mouth of Chesapeake Bay, decided to steal a nearby boat and sail it across the harbor to Fort Monroe, which was in Union hands. They surrendered to General Benjamin Butler, the Union commander, who allowed them to stay in the fort and declared them contraband (property) of war. Butler was a lawyer in civilian life, and understood that in the rules of warfare, if an enemy intended to use any kind of property to wage war, the opposing side could claim it as contraband of war if captured. These three men were slaves, thus property, who were forced to build fortifications to be used against the Union, so declaring them as contraband was a reasonable solution. These three men opened a floodgate of enslaved people fleeing to Union lines, and by the end of the war, some 500,000 people used this avenue of escape.

The Civil War continued into 1862, and early that year, much of the action took place in the western theater. A Union commander named Ulysses S. Grant won two Union victories in Tennessee by capturing Confederate forts Henry and Donelson. By April, Grant was poised to attack and capture the Confederate railroad junction at Corinth, Mississippi. But unbeknownst to him, the Confederate commander, Albert Sydney Johnston—considered by many to be the finest Confederate general—had moved his army out of Corinth, and had snuck in behind Grant's army at Pittsburg Landing on the Tennessee River, near a small church called Shiloh. Early on the morning of April 6, he unleashed his forces, and for

Union forces recapture artillery at the Battle of Shiloh, 1886 engraving.

Confederate generals: Jefferson Davis in a red cloak is at center left; Robert E. Lee with a saber is at center right.

The South Builds an Army

What the South lacked in resources, it made up for in enthusiasm. In the excitement of secession, Southern men rushed to form units, fearing the war would be over quickly. The Confederacy was hampered, however, by lacking an established government. Nevertheless, Jefferson Davis had been secretary of war, and Leroy Walker, Davis's secretary of war, was an honest and capable administrator, so the creation of the armed forces began well. Being in the position of defending their homes and lands lent an additional urgency to the South's efforts. State militias proved to be the backbone of the Southern military effort. The South was also fortunate to have officers like Josiah Gorgas, Isaac St. John, and George Rains who supplied their armies with ordnance. Though most senior officers had been trained at West Point, the thousands of officers in the lower grades were lawyers, farmers, or capable individuals who rose through the ranks. Though surviving Confederate records are incomplete, historians estimate that 500,000 to two million men served their country.

hours, the Confederates pounded the Union position, driving them almost into the Tennessee River.

The next day, Union reinforcements arrived, and pushed the Confederates off the field, winning an important victory. Shiloh was significant as a Union victory, but the loss of life was staggering. In two days, there was a total of more than 23,000 casualties. Manassas had seemed like a slaughtering pen with its 5,000 casualties; it paled in comparison to Shiloh. Americans, both in the North and in the South, had difficulty fathoming the loss of life.

The war continued through 1862, and the bloodbath at Shiloh became the norm rather than the exception. In the East, in September, the Confederate and Union armies clashed in Maryland, near a stream called Antietam. The casualties in this one-day battle equaled the two-day total at Shiloh, making this the bloodiest day in American history. But the significance of Antietam went well beyond the loss of life. From the beginning of the war, the Confederacy had vainly hoped that England and France might recognize the Confederate states and support its war effort. Historians have debated whether or not this was a possibility, but if it ever was possible, with the Union victory at Antietam, any chance of that recognition ended.

The Battle of Antietam, September 17, 1862.

For several months, President Lincoln had been struggling with the idea that in addition to reuniting the Union, ending slavery should be another war aim. Antietam was just barely a Union victory, but it was all Lincoln needed to issue his Emancipation Proclamation. He proclaimed that if the Confederates did not surrender by the end of 1862, all enslaved people in the Confederate states would be free on January 1, 1863. Of course, he had no way of enforcing this order, since the Confederates were still fighting and had no intention of freeing their slaves, but it symbolically made the end of slavery a war aim.

Not long after the Emancipation Proclamation went into effect, the Union army began recruiting African American soldiers into its ranks. Several black regiments had already formed, but now there was a concerted effort to recruit blacks into the army and navy. By the end of the war, some 200,000 African American soldiers and sailors served, and most were former slaves. Frederick Douglass, himself a former slave and a leader in the American antislavery movement, said, "let the black man get upon his person the brass letters U.S., let him get an eagle on his button, and a musket on his shoulder, and bullets in his pocket, and there is no power on earth or under the earth which can deny that he has earned the right of citizenship in the United States." These soldiers were not uncertain about what they were fighting for; they were fighting to end slavery.

African Americans were not the only ethnic group to fight in the Civil War. Regiments of Irish and Germans were engaged, as well as Chinese and Pacific Islanders sprinkled mostly throughout the Union army. Jewish soldiers fought on both sides. More than 20,000 American Indians fought as well—on both sides—and in some cases members of the same nation fought against each other. Such was the case in the Battle of Honey Springs, fought in Indian Territory (present-day Oklahoma), on June 17, 1863. It was unique as the largest, and perhaps the only Civil War battle in which white soldiers, on both sides, were in the minority. American Indians fought on both sides. Cherokees and Creeks made up the majority of American Indian soldiers on the Confederate side, as well as Choctaws and Chickasaws. The Cherokees and Creeks also fought on the Union side, joined by companies of Seminole, Shawnee, Delaware, Keechi, Caddo, Kickapoo, and Osage tribes, as well as soldiers from other smaller tribes. In addition, African American soldiers from the 1st Kansas Colored Infantry fought on the Union side.

The carnage continued. Confederate General Robert E. Lee won major victories at Fredericksburg and Chancellorsville, Virginia, and decided to invade the North. At the tiny crossroads town of Gettysburg, Pennsylvania, Lee was defeated in the bloodiest battle yet (over 53,000 casualties) and forced to retreat back into Virginia. On July 4, 1863, General Grant

Thomas Nast's illustration celebrating the emancipation of Southern slaves.

captured Vicksburg, which gave the Union control of the Mississippi River and isolated Arkansas, Louisiana, and Texas from the rest of the Confederacy. From then until the end of the war in April 1865, the war became one of attrition. The Union armies steadily defeated Confederate armies at Chattanooga and Atlanta, and pinned down Lee's army in the siege of Petersburg and Richmond, while Sherman captured Atlanta and "marched to the sea" through the heart of Georgia.

Quite unlike the "bloodless war" some envisioned at the beginning, the Civil War was anything but bloodless. There were more than 10,000 engagements from as far west as Arizona to as far east as the coast of France—near Cherbourg—where the Union ship *Kearsarge* sank the Confederate ship *Alabama*. The Confederates even took the war into the North Pacific Ocean, where the CSS *Shenandoah* captured and burned a

The Confederate charge against Union forces at Gettysburg, illustration by A.R. Waud.

number of American whaling vessels. In perhaps the most bizarre episode in the war, on October 19, 1864, in the small town of St. Albans, Vermont, Confederate soldiers disguised as civilians robbed the town's three banks of over $200,000, then fled to Canada.

The End of the War and Reconstruction

The Civil War ended when General Robert E. Lee surrendered to General Ulysses S. Grant on April 9, 1865, at Appomattox Court House, Virginia. President Lincoln was assassinated just six days later.

Initially, the new president, Andrew Johnson, tried to allow the former Confederate states to return to the Union without the institution of slavery, but with nearly everything else intact. Unhappy with Johnson's approach, Congress established its own Reconstruction program, including passage of the 14th and 15th Amendments to the Constitution. Congressional Reconstruction was remarkably creative and progressive. Former slaves

The Tale of Wilmer McLean

A merchant by the name of Wilmer McLean lived with his family on a small farm in Virginia. When the Confederate army established its defensive position along Bull Run, McLean offered his house to the commander, Brigadier General P. T. G. Beauregard. During the skirmish, both sides traded artillery salvos, and one of the Union shells sailed through McLean's house. McLean's barn was used as a hospital for Confederate wounded. The cornerstone from McLean's barn is on exhibit in Manassas National Battlefield Park. So, it could be said that the Civil War started in Wilmer McLean's house and barn.

About four years later, McLean had moved his business and family about 120 miles south and west of Manassas to a quiet hamlet called Appomattox Court House. In early April 1865, the war again visited Wilmer McLean and his family. On April 8, a messenger from Confederate General Robert E. Lee knocked on McLean's door and informed him that Lee wished to use his house to surrender to Lieutenant General Ulysses S. Grant, effectively ending the Civil War. The next day, Grant and his officers and Lee and his officers gathered in McLean's parlor for the formal surrender. McLean was reported to have said, "the war began in my front yard and ended in my front parlor." The McLean House is now part of Appomattox Court House National Historical Park.

The McLean House at Appomattox Court House.

General Grant and troops storm Fort Donelson. 1862 lithograph by Currier & Ives.

The Cost of War

The firing on Fort Sumter unleashed unimaginable human and financial destruction. Four years later, nearly 1.5 million Americans were killed, wounded, captured, or missing. Some historians suggest as many as 750,000 died. The previous estimate of 620,000 dead includes 360,000 Union and 260,000 Confederate troops. Two thirds died from disease, accidents, suicide, murder, or execution. The financial costs are equally staggering. In 1861, the Federal budget totaled $80.2 million and included $36.4 million for defense; the comparable figures in 1865 were $1.33 billion and $1.17 billion. By war's end, the accumulated Federal deficit had grown from $90.6 million in 1861 to $2.68 billion in 1865. The Federal government spent $6.19 billion prosecuting the war, and another $3.3 billion for veterans' pensions by 1906. The estimated cost to the Confederacy was $2.1 billion. Far harder to estimate are the costs of the physical and economic devastation to the South, which took a century to recover, and the price paid by African Americans who were prevented from realizing the war's promise of equality for just as long.

flocked to the free public schools hungry to learn. In some areas, they were allowed to own and farm their own land. A number of African Americans, including some former slaves, were elected to public office, including the U.S. Congress. And, to ensure that these programs were carried out with as little interference as possible, the military was stationed in areas in which there was a potential for violence.

Southern whites lost the war and lost their slaves, but they managed to reestablish a semblance of their former society where blacks were relegated to inferior social, economic, and political status. Eventually, through violence—by the way of the Ku Klux Klan or other illegal organizations—they gained back their power as Congress withdrew troops from the South and revoked much of the mechanism for Reconstruction. The U.S. Supreme Court liberally interpreted the 14th and 15th Amendments, removing protections for blacks. It would take nearly a century before African Americans were able to enjoy the fruits of the "new birth of freedom" promised to them from the Civil War.

Lee surrenders to Grant on April 9, 1865, 1867 painting by Louis Guillaume.

Civil War reenactors at Kennesaw Mountain National Battlefield Park.

Legacy of the Civil War

Few topics in American history have captured the interest of Americans, or for that matter, people in other countries, than our Civil War. A popular online book service currently lists over 20,000 books under the heading "American Civil War." Civil War reenactments take place all over the country, and within this community, reenactors are separated into groups.

The United States military, and for that matter, military from around the world travel to Civil War battlefields to study the battles. They are able to do this, because over 100 years ago, veterans from both sides of the war joined forces to push Congress to set aside as federal parks the sacred ground on which they had earlier tried to kill each other. There are currently over 20 Civil War battlefields managed by the National Park Service where visitors can see not only where the war was fought, but also learn what caused the war, how the battles affected the soldiers who fought the war, its impact on families, and its impact on our nation.

The American Civil War was the most momentous era in American history. It defined who we are as a nation, both then and now. In 1861, racial slavery kept nearly four million black Americans in bondage. Slavery claimed the protection of the Constitution and was legal in 15 states as well as in the District of Columbia. This "peculiar institution," based on human property, shaped the economy, society, politics, and ideology of the Union. The Civil War decided, once and for all, both the question of slavery and of citizenship. The 13th Amendment prohibited slavery, while the 14th and 15th Amendments defined and nationalized citizenship and banned race as a reason for depriving people of their rights of citizenship. Repealing any of these amendments or a return to an unfree labor system is unthinkable today.

Viewed in these terms, the Civil War era saw not only our greatest military struggle, but also our greatest social revolution and our greatest evolution as a nation. Granted, after 150 years we still struggle to define our concept of citizenship, and to meet Abraham Lincoln's challenge of "a new birth of freedom," but this debate would not even take place without the American Civil War.

A postcard ca. 1900 commemorates those who fought in the Civil War.

Following is a partial list of the Civil War sites that are preserved by the National Park Service.

Andersonville National Historic Site, Andersonville, Georgia. On the site of the Civil War-era prison camp, this park commemorates the sacrifices by prisoners in the 1861-65 conflict and in all wars in which the United States has fought.

Andersonville NHS

Antietam National Battlefield, Sharpsburg, Maryland. The Army of Northern Virginia's first invasion of the North (1862) ended here. The Union victory gave Lincoln the opportunity to issue the Emancipation Proclamation.

Appomattox Court House National Historical Park, Appomattox, Virginia. In this small village, Robert E. Lee surrendered the Army of Northern Virginia to Ulysses S. Grant in April 1865.

Arlington House, The Robert E. Lee Memorial, Arlington, Virginia. Arlington House was the home of Robert E. Lee's wife. The house and lands were seized early in the war and used for Union burials. Today, it is Arlington National Cemetery.

Brices Cross Roads National Battlefield Site, Tupelo, Mississippi. Union and Confederate forces clashed here on the supply line between Nashville and Chattanooga.

Cedar Creek and Belle Grove National Historical Park, Middletown, Virginia. In October 1864, the Confederates achieved what seemed to be a great victory. Union General Philip Sheridan rallied his troops and soundly defeated the Confederates.

Chickamauga and Chattanooga National Military Park, Fort Oglethorpe, Georgia. The Confederates won a great victory at Chickamauga, but two months later, Union victories in Chattanooga prepared the way for Sherman's march on Atlanta.

Chickamauga and Chattanooga NMP

Ford's Theatre National Historic Site, Washington, D.C. This is the theater in which Abraham Lincoln was shot, April 14, 1865. Across the street is the Petersen House where the mortally wounded president died the next morning.

Fort Donelson National Battlefield, Dover, Tennessee. Grant's victory here in February 1862, opened the Tennessee and Cumberland rivers to Union gunboats and steamers. His success gave the North a new hero.

Fort Pulaski NM

Fort Pulaski National Monument,

Savannah, Georgia. This massive brick fort took 18 years to build, but in 1862, the newly developed rifled cannon blasted through the brickwork, making brick fortifications obsolete.

Fort Sumter National Monument,

Charleston, South Carolina. On April 12, 1861, Confederate batteries around Charleston harbor opened fire on the Federal garrison in the fort. It was the first engagement of the Civil War.

Fort Sumter NM

Fredericksburg and Spotsylvania County Battlefields Memorial National Military Park, Fredericksburg, Virginia.

This park contains four major Civil War battlefields: Fredericksburg, Chancellors-ville, the Wilderness, and Spotsylvania Court House.

Gettysburg National Military Park,

Gettysburg, Pennsylvania. The battle fought here July 1–3, 1863, was an important Union victory and ended Lee's second attempt to invade the North.

Harpers Ferry National Historical Park,

Harpers Ferry, West Virginia. John Brown attacked the Federal arsenal here, believing he could take weapons, arm the slaves, and begin an uprising. However, he was captured, tried for treason, and hanged.

Kennesaw Mountain National Battlefield Park, Kennesaw, Georgia. In

1864, Confederate General Joseph E. Johnston mounted a stalwart defense and temporarily stopped Sherman's advance on Atlanta.

Manassas National Battlefield Park,

Manassas, Virginia. Both the first (1861) and second (1862) battle of Manassas were fought over this ground. The first battle gave the South the confidence to continue, and the second showed both sides that the war would not end soon.

Manassas NBP

Pea Ridge National Military Park, Pea

Ridge, Arkansas. The Union victory here, in one of the few battles west of the Mississippi, ensured that Missouri would remain with the Union. Cherokees, Choctaws, and Chickasaws fought with the Confederates.

Pea Ridge NMP

Petersburg National Battlefield, Petersburg, Virginia. Miles of trenches recall the 10-month siege of this vital rail center. When Grant broke through Confederate lines in spring 1865, the Confederates evacuated Petersburg and Richmond.

Richmond National Battlefield Park, Richmond, Virginia. Richmond was the capital of the Confederacy and a major manufacturing center for the South. A number of battles took place over the years before the final evacuation in 1865.

Richmond NBP

Shiloh National Military Park, Shiloh, Tennessee. The rail junction at Corinth, Mississippi, was the target of Grant's advance in the spring of 1862. The battle was a draw, but the Union soon secured Corinth, disrupting Confederate supply lines.

Shiloh NMP

Stones River National Battlefield, Murfreesboro, Tennessee. A bitter battle, December 31, 1862 to January 2, 1863, took place here for control of middle Tennessee. Though both sides suffered terribly from the fighting, the Confederates were the ones who withdrew.

Tupelo National Battlefield, Tupelo, Mississippi. Here in July 1864, Nathan Bedford Forrest tried, and failed, to cut the rail line that was supplying Sherman's march on Atlanta.

Vicksburg National Military Park, Vicksburg, Mississippi. The siege of this vital river port ended in Union success one day after the victory at Gettysburg. This battle gave the Union complete control of the Mississippi River, and the Confederacy was cut in two.

Vicksburg NMP

Wilson's Creek National Battlefield, Republic, Missouri. On August 10, 1861, Union and Confederate forces met here in the first battle west of the Mississippi River. The Union victory meant that this important slave state would stay in the Union.

To read more about the Civil War and our national parks, please visit www.nps.gov.